Cecilia Weather's was born in Arbroath, Scotland on 18th of October 1952. She is the second eldest of six children. Cecilia wrote poetry from a young age and still does. She wrote this story after sending her husband's CV for a job without telling him. It is based almost exactly on what happened, which wasn't funny for her husband at the time, but, has caused many friends to laugh and encourage her to write the story. She hopes you enjoy it too.

I would like to dedicate this book to Timothy, my dear husband of 48 years. He is a very patient, caring man, always wanting to please. He is the father of my five children. He has positively encouraged me to write this story even though it caused him all sorts of problems on the day.

Cecilia Weathers

THE INTERVIEW

AUSTIN MACAULEY PUBLISHERS™

LONDON • CAMBRIDGE • NEW YORK • SHARJAH

A CIP catalogue record for this title is available from the British Library.

ISBN 9781398493230 (Paperback)
ISBN 9781398493247 (ePub e-book)

www.austinmacauley.com

First Published 2023
Austin Macauley Publishers Ltd®
1 Canada Square
Canary Wharf
London
E14 5AA

I would like to thank the Austin Macauley Publishers for their assistance in the book reaching publication.

"For crying out loud," Lucy yelled, "I can't believe it." She played the answer phone again and listened, her mind going into sheer panic. *'What had she done? How would Sam feel when he heard what she'd done?'* She put the phone down, rubbed her chin and started pacing the room; something she always did when she was anxious.

Lucy, who had just arrived home after a long day of teaching in a large comprehensive school had been looking forward to putting her feet up with a large mug of coffee and the local paper she'd picked up on the way home. It was a job she loved and had had for the past two years since moving down to live in Eastbourne with her husband, Sam. Unfortunately, Sam had not been so lucky with his job; working in maintenance at a care home. He was always moaning about not being appreciated, and how much work they expected him to do.

Lucy always felt sorry for him and tried to comfort him by saying that everyone had something about their job that they didn't like. Sam was sadly one of those people who was never satisfied with any job he had. He was a bit of a moaner. Lucy put up with it though as he was a wonderful husband who she loved very much. He was always telling her he loved her, buying her flowers, cooking her meals and many other things.

They had three children that had all flown the nest. Jack, aged twenty-seven, the oldest, was tall like his dad and had the same attitude towards work. Jack had always complained about anything and everything. He'd trained at college to be a chef. He'd since been a barman, worked on the roads tarmacking and run a café. Now at last he had seemed to find his niche in life. After winning some money on the lottery, he had started his own business as a baker and for the past two years, had built his business up, creating amazing cakes for weddings, birthdays and other functions. Being self-employed meant he had no one to complain to or about. At last, he had moved out of home and although he often came around, he seemed to stand on his own two feet.

Millie was twenty-five and was now a primary school teacher in London. She had had a more serious outlook on life, had loved spending long evenings after school and then college, studying into the early hours. At weekends, she dressed herself up and let her long blonde hair loose, then set off with her friends to the local nightclubs to relax and enjoy herself.

Her younger sister, Emma, aged twenty, was an actress and also lived in London. Emma had gone to drama school and loved every bit. She was loud and funny and with her olive skin and dark-curly hair, attracted men at the turn of a hat. She enjoyed mixing with the stars and the up-and-coming actors like herself, partying late into the night.

Lucy once again thought how she'd tell Sam and pressed play on the phone once more, putting it on loudspeaker this time.

"Good morning, Mr Jones. This is Jesus College in Oxford. We sent you an email at the beginning of last week, after short listing you for an interview for the post of caretaker you'd applied for. As we hadn't heard from you, we thought we would phone and see if you're still interested. Please ring as soon as possible to let us know, as your interview is this Friday the 13th at twelve thirty."

That was only three days away! Why hadn't I told him I'd sent off for the job, Lucy thought. *He's going to be livid.* Lucy over the years had often sent off for jobs for Sam, but she'd always discussed it with him first. *If he wasn't so darned disagreeable about his work, she wouldn't feel obliged to find him a new one all the time,* she argued with herself.

She got out her laptop to refresh herself about the job being offered. Caretaker with experience wanted for Jesus College, Oxford. He had lots of experience as he'd been caretaker of a school for eight years, and the salary they offered was good as well. To be truthful, the two bedroomed house with a garden that came with the job had attracted her to it. She loved Oxford. Her sister lived there with her family right on the river's edge. They had a punt moored there and often took them up the river when they visited. It was idyllic.

Now she had to sell it to Sam. He loathed interviews, and after each one swore, he'd never do another. The longest job had been one he'd held for eight years as a caretaker in a primary school in Pangbourne. He had been his own boss, and it had come with a lovely three-bedroomed house in the grounds. Lucy had got a job there after a year as a teacher. All had been great until Sam's brother, Pete, who lived in Wales, had phoned to say he had to have a serious operation. They had both felt it was time to help look after his mum. Pete, who was her carer, wouldn't be able to take that job back on for at least six months. So off they'd gone, after giving a month's notice; leaving most of their goods in storage. Lucy, who always loved a new challenge, said he'd be able to get a job easily, and she'd mind his mother. When they'd got there, his mother was very confused. She kept calling Sam, Pete. He kept saying he was Sam and not Pete, his brother. She had dementia and couldn't remember Sam. Poor Lucy had not understood things were going to be so difficult.

"Mum," she said, "you must remember Sam. He's your youngest son."

"What a load of rubbish," she'd answered. "I only have one son, and that's Pete. Who are you?" Mum had asked. "What are you doing in my house? Get out or I'll call the police."

"I'm your daughter-in-law, Lucy," she'd answered in despair. "I'm married to Sam, your other son. Look, here's a picture of us with our children, your grandchildren," she'd said, showing her a photograph that she'd taken off her mantel piece.

"Oh yes, I remember now. That's Jack, Millie and Emma," she'd said in a rare lucid moment, holding on to the photo with an enormous smile on her face, "but who are you?"

"Look, that's me, Lucy," she'd said, pointing at herself, "and that's Sam, your younger son, my husband."

"It's all very complicated," she sighed. "I don't seem to remember much nowadays."

"No problem. We will help while Pete goes to hospital. You haven't seen us for ages, that's why you've forgotten who we are. We're going to stay for six months, so you'll soon get used to having us around."

That six months had turned out to be rather harrowing. Sam couldn't find a job, so Lucy had gone to work as a supply teacher in a local school. Of course, at night she'd get home to lots of moans and groans about how difficult it was, looking after his mother. How she'd wander off when he'd taken her down to the village shopping, how she refused to eat what he cooked for her, how she had insisted on baking Pete's favourite cakes and the mess she'd left for him to clean up.

"I wouldn't mind," he'd said, "but I am her son. There's only two of us. Why doesn't she remember me?"

Once again, she'd try to pacify him by saying, "You're doing such a wonderful job and she has got dementia."

Six months later, they couldn't wait to leave. Pete's operation had gone well. He had made a full recovery and was now ready to take on his job as mum's carer once again.

So, they had moved on a whim to Eastbourne, which is where they lived now. Lucy, who had always wanted to live by the sea on the south coast, was delighted when Sam had agreed. They'd rented a furnished flat to settle down in while they looked for jobs. They soon found they liked it in Eastbourne. Sadly, Sam was always complaining about his job, so a month ago, Lucy had sent his CV to a job she'd found on the internet and hadn't given it another thought. That was until today.

Crumbs. What will he say? she thought.

Lucy picked up the phone. Her hands were sweaty, she felt anxious.

She'd thought and thought about what to say, and it wasn't getting any easier or clearer. She just had to get on with it.

"Hello darling, it's Lucy."

"Hi, it's not like you to phone at this time of day. Do you need me to bring something back from Sainsbury?"

"No, no. I just got back from work and found a message on the phone to you."

"Oh, what was it?"

"Well, it was from Jesus College in Oxford, asking if you'd like to come for an interview."

"An interview? What do you mean an interview?"

"Well, a month ago, when you kept moaning about your job, I started searching the caretaker's website for you."

"But you never mentioned it to me, don't you think you should have?"

Lucy felt that sinking feeling she got when she felt guilty about something.

"I know. I thought you might worry about it or feel depressed if you didn't get an interview. I'm really sorry I didn't discuss it with you first."

"For crying out loud, when is this interview meant to be?"

"That's the problem, Sam, it's on Friday."

"This Friday? Do you know that's in two days' time; and worse still, it'll be Friday the 13th?" he yelled down the phone.

Lucy's stomach dropped even further and left her with a sick feeling. She curled up on the sofa with tears in her eyes. He never got angry with her, not to mention she hadn't even thought about the date. He'd always been superstitious about Friday the 13th.

"I know. I can't believe it myself. To be quite honest, I'd totally forgotten about the job. Could you get Friday off? It's a great job, with good pay, and comes with a house in the grounds."

"I'll have to think about it. You haven't exactly given me much time, have you?"

"But they want you to get back to them today, with a yes or no about the interview," she pleaded, feeling a right heel.

"Look, I'll ask my manager right now and get back to you. OK?"

"OK. I'm really sorry. I honestly forgot about sending your CV."

While she was waiting to hear from him, Lucy got on the internet and printed out a map of Oxford, showing the college and the railway station. She then got a red pen and penned in the best way for him to get there from the station. Then she googled trainline to figure out the best route and time for leaving to get there in plenty of time. Just then, the phone rang.

"I've got Friday off by telling them I had some business to attend to and as I had time owing, they allowed it. I must have caught her on a good day."

"OK, that's great. Would you like me to email them back with a yes, that you will attend the interview? Shall I buy a train ticket for you online?"

"Yes, to both. I'll speak to you about this when I get home."

"OK. I'm getting on to it right away," Lucy replied, feeling better about the whole thing. *Making his favourite supper will cheer him up,* she thought, getting up to get out the ingredients for a beef stew. *I'll also make his favourite sweet syrup pudding. That should make him more amenable,* she sighed, pulling a bottle of red out of the wine rack as an afterthought.

An hour later, Sam arrived home a bit disgruntled, but smelling the stew cooking, he accepted a glass of red wine and soon cheered up.

"Well, show me the job description," he asked. "I want to know everything about it, and especially if I qualify for it."

"You do, darling. I would never send for something that was unsuitable. You have lots of experience and that's what they want. Your time keepings good, you always keep things tidy, you know all about health and safety, so the job sounds right up your street. Here, look at the job description on the internet," she said, pointing to the laptop on her desk.

He sat down at the desk and read it through. A few minutes later, she saw him physically relax. "It looks good," he said, downing the rest of his wine in one go and holding it out to be filled again. She took it from him; went back to the kitchen, dished out the stew and tatties, poured the glass full again and one for herself, put them on a tray and took them through to the dining table.

"Dinners ready," she called. "Come on, it'll get cold. You can study that later."

"Alright, I'm coming," he replied, walking into the room. "Wow, that looks good, my favourite. You trying to get around me or something?"

"Well, I felt such a heel not talking to you about it. But to be quite honest, it was a month ago, and I'd totally forgotten."

"Never do that again. It's totally freaked me out."

"I won't. Look, I've printed out a map and put a red line in to show you the quickest way from the station. I've also found a train that will get you in, in plenty of time. I'm afraid it's two changes, one at Gatwick, one at Reading. Pretty simple if you get on and off at the times I've put down. Each stop gives you plenty of time to get on the next train."

After a pleasant supper, they settled down to talk about Oxford. They'd been there often to visit Lucy's family when they'd lived in Pangbourne. Lucy loved Oxford's beautiful city of stunning architecture, history and culture, with its ancient and modern colleges, fascinating museums and galleries, plenty of parks, gardens and green spaces to relax. Her enthusiasm spilt over as always and got Sam excited about the prospect too.

"What about giving your beard a cut?" Lucy asked.

"Why do you think it needs cutting?"

"Well, it definitely needs tidying up and will take years off you which will help when you're going for an interview at fifty-six."

"Alright. You better give my hair a trim too."

Lucy got her scissors, electric razor and comb out, put a towel around his neck and started on the beard first. It was amazing how much younger he looked with it cut short. Then she set to on his hair. It was receding at the front and thinning there too. As she worked her way around his head, suddenly the attachment jumped off the electric razor and she found she'd shaved a patch at the back down to the skin. She stopped, bent down to retrieve the piece that had fallen onto the floor, and stifled a giggle. 'Crumbs. What could she do? It was almost as large as a fifty pence piece. He'd be furious with her.'

"What's wrong?" Sam asked.

"Nothing," she replied, stifling a huge, nervous giggle by placing her hand over her mouth.

"What are you laughing at?"

"Well, the attachment on the razor flew off and I've shaved a tiny piece of your hair very short. I'll be able to cover it with something, don't worry."

"You stupid idiot!" he yelled. "How can I go to an interview with a piece of my hair missing?"

"It's a tiny piece, really. I'll be able to cover it with some shoe polish."

"Shoe polish?" he yelled. "Are you having a joke?"

"Well no. Your hair is reddish, and a light tan would cover the patch beautifully," Lucy replied.

"Get the mirror and let me see what you've done to me."

"It's small, really. It wasn't my fault the stupid attachment flew off, so I don't know why you're shouting at me."

"I'm not shouting at you. I'm just upset at being scalped."

"You're not scalped. I can cover it up. It's really quite small," she snapped back. "Look," she said, holding the mirror up behind his head while he looked in another mirror. "It's not so bad, is it?"

"Hmmmm, I suppose not," he replied, feeling it with his hand. "Try the shoe polish on it and let me see."

"Okay," Lucy agreed quickly, going through to the kitchen to get it from under the sink. She rubbed some on his patch, and it really made a difference. "Look," she said, "I told you it wouldn't show."

Picking the mirror back up and staring at it from all angles, he had to agree it wasn't too bad.

"Now, let's give you a brush down, and then you can go up and relax in a nice hot bath."

The next day, Sam went to work and expected someone to mention the bare patch on his head, but luckily, no one did.

When he arrived home that evening, he found Lucy had bought a delicious Chinese meal on her way home from work and had put it in the oven to keep warm. Chicken chow mein, sweet and sour chicken balls and egg fried rice. She'd also bought a lemon cheesecake to round off the meal.

"So, I've printed off the map and details of your journey. The train leaves at seven twenty-six, gets into Gatwick at eight fifty; leaves Gatwick at three minutes past nine, gets into Reading at ten fifteen; and then leaves Reading at ten forty and arrives in Oxford at eleven ten. This gives you plenty of time to make your way to the college for the interview at twelve thirty. I've put all your health and safety, fire awareness, control of substances hazards to health, and moving and handling certificates in with references and your latest CV. I've also typed out a load of questions and answers they might ask, for you to study before you get there. I've put them all inside this," she said, handing him a new yellow ochre folder.

After looking at all the things Lucy had thought to put in, he said, "Thanks so much. It will really help to go over all of these things before I get there, especially the questions and answers they may ask."

"Great, I'm glad to be of help, seeing as I'm the one who put you in this position."

"Come here," he said, pulling her into his arms. "I'm sorry I was in a foul mood yesterday, but you gave me such a shock. I'm looking forward to it now. It'll be great working on my own again and living in the centre of Oxford." He cuddled up to her and suggested an early night.

"Okay. Just let me put the dishes in the sink and tidy everything away then I'll be up."

"No, I'll do that. You go up first and take a bottle up with you and a couple of clean glasses," he said, handing her a fresh bottle of their favourite tipple.

"Okay, if you're sure," she said, and scampered off upstairs to the bedroom. She felt so happy that he was happy, and that he was even looking forward to going now.

After a wonderful evening together, Sam set the clock for six a.m. and Lucy told him she would go with him to the station in the morning to see him off.

Next morning after breakfast, she handed him a bag with a hot flask of tea for the journey and a few nibbles to eat. At the station she bought him a newspaper, knowing he'd be reading the sports pages at the back.

"Best of luck, darling. Remember to check the stops. It's easy enough. I've written it all down for you. It's in the folder. Here are your tickets. For crying out loud, don't lose them."

"I won't," he said, "stop fussing." Pulling her to him, he kissed her and said, "I love you and I'll see you tonight. Stop worrying."

"Remember to phone me after the interview," she called as he went through the barrier.

"Yes, of course I will," he blew her a kiss as the train pulled away.

Lucy went home as it was still too early to go to school.

Sam got on the train. It surprised him that it was so full, but on consideration thought it must be commuters or people on their way to Gatwick for an early morning flight. He plonked himself down by a window, and soon someone was sitting next to him. On the other side of the table were two youngsters, totally engrossed in themselves. They had rings on their lips, noses, ears, and eyebrows. There was an assortment of tattoos on their arms and necks. Their clothes were mostly black, with studs dotted here and there, and their hair had been dyed black too. He thought they might be Goths.

It fascinated him the way they dressed and appeared, not giving a care to what people thought of them. The girl brought out an iPhone, tuned it on to some awful music then plugged some earphones into it which she shared with her partner. Even though her earphones were in, he could still hear the music and wondered if it would damage her hearing in later life.

Why did youngsters not realise that their loud music disturbed others, he thought, looking around to see if there were any other seats empty. He spotted two at the end of the carriage and, grabbing his carrier bag, excused himself and made his way down the train. Just before he got there, two other people sat in the vacant seats.

Blast, he thought, *why didn't I just stay where I was?* Looking, he saw that the seat he'd vacated was now filled, so he made his way into the next carriage and luckily found the only seat left, by the toilet. There was a rather scruffy, middle-aged, plump man sitting by the window. His clothes were filthy and smelly. He had long greasy hair and an unkempt beard that had bits of old food stuck in it.

"Mornin," he said, smiling and showing a set of rotten teeth. "Goin' anywhere special like or just off to work?"

"Just off to work," Sam replied, hoping that if he pulled out his flask and poured himself a cup of tea, the man might leave him alone.

"Looks good an' 'ot. Got enough for a small un?" he asked Sam.

"Sorry, I've only got one cup, otherwise I'd be happy to give you some," he replied.

"I don't mind sharin', if you don't," the man said, "the name's 'Arry." He smiled, holding out his hand.

"Hi, the name's Sam. Look, you have it Harry," he said, passing him the cup. "I had one just before I set off this morning."

"You sure, mate, it's awful kind of you, thank you very much," he laughed, taking it and slurping it down.

Sam sighed and settled down, wishing yet again that he hadn't moved. *Maybe Harry would get off in Eastbourne,* he thought.

"Cor me feet don' 'alf ache," said Harry, reaching down and pulling off his boots. "Got bunions," he said, pulling off one of his filthy, holey socks.

The rancid whiff of unwashed feet filled the surrounding air. The smell was unbearable. Sam nearly gagged and hurriedly said he had to go to the toilet. As he shut the door of the loo, he sat down and pondered on his morning. He wasn't even halfway there yet and everything had been a nightmare so far. *Please God, let him get off soon,* he thought. *I can't bear another minute of that smell.* Just then, it came over the Tannoy that they were approaching Eastbourne. If Harry got off, he'd move down the train again once people had vacated their seats. He waited until the train stopped, then peaked out of the door. Harry had gone.

The carriage was about half full now. He looked around and saw a single seat all on its own. He quickly recovered his mug, flask, and bag, then put them onto the pull-down table in front of his seat and sat down. *Please, Lord, may there be no more distractions.* The train filled up again and Sam settled down to look in his folder. He pulled out a few things and came across a lovely card from Lucy, wishing him good luck. A warm feeling of deep love and appreciation came over him and filled his heart. *She really was something,* he reflected,

22

*always remembering the little things that would make him feel
good.*

All was quiet until they reached Lewes, where a family of
five got on. They were obviously going on holiday as the poor
dad was trying to fit several suitcases into an already full rack.
Mum tried to pile the children into a four-seater with a table
in the middle. It was just in front of Sam.

"I don't want to sit next to him," cried one child, pointing
to his brother.

"Just sit where you're told," Mum said in a very firm
voice.

"But I don't want to," the child repeated.

"If you don't sit down where you're told, we won't go on
holiday. We'll get off at the next stop and get a train home. Is
that what you want?" Mum asked.

Everything went quiet, and Dad, eventually free of the
cases, came and joined them all.

"Well, they're obedient children," he said, oblivious to the
row that had just finished. "Just think, we'll all be up in the
sky on an aeroplane soon. Exciting, eh?"

"Dad, will we see the clouds?" asked one of his brood.

"Yes, when we get high enough, you'll be going through
them and then above them. They just look like huge cotton
wool balls. You'll love it."

"Will we see God up in the clouds?" asked another.

"I'm not sure. He might be there; or he may be somewhere
else today. It's an enormous world, you know."

"What about angels?" the child persisted.

"I honestly don't know. We can look and see. Now, how
about a game of snap?" he said, trying to change the subject
while pulling out a pack of cards.

A noisy game ensued, but not so bad as to annoy Sam. He sat reminiscing about the first holiday he had had by plane, and how excited he'd been. He closed his eyes and remembered how his own thoughts had been like there's. The dad was right. It was amazing going through and above the clouds, and they had looked just like cotton wool. He loved flying. With that, he fell into a deep, dreamy sleep.

The next thing he knew, the train jolted him awake as it started up again. He looked out of the window and saw a Gatwick airport sign go by.

Flaming heck, he thought, *what an idiot I am, I'll never get to the interview on time.*

Pulling out his mobile, he tried to phone Lucy. She wouldn't pick up.

Blast, he said to himself. He looked at his watch and thought, *she'll be in class until ten, and then there would be a ten-minute slot he could contact her in as she changed classrooms.*

I'll just have to get off at the next stop and go back to Gatwick. What a stupid, stupid idiot I am. He looked up to find out the name of the next station and found it to be Horley. Collecting his things together, he sat very awake now, listening for Horley to be announced. *How long had she given him at Oxford to get to the college,* he wondered. *She had said plenty of time.* He pulled out the papers from his folder with times and instructions on it and found he had had an hour and twenty minutes, so he might still get there on time. It all depended on the connections.

"The next station will be Horley. Please remember to take all your luggage with you. We wish you a safe onward journey."

Sam quickly got himself to the door and soon found himself on the platform. He saw a bridge in the distance he had to cross to get over to the other side, so made his way towards it. When he got to the other side, he looked up to see the next train back to Gatwick. It would be in fifteen minutes. He looked at his watch. It had taken two minutes to get here, so that would be nineteen minutes of time wasted. He would miss his connection to Reading.

Damn, he swore to himself. *I better not phone Lucy or she'll be worried.* He got out his phone and phoned through to the college.

"Hello, Jesus College, can I help you?"

"Hello, I'm coming for an interview today and will probably not make my slot for twelve thirty."

"So, you won't be on time then?"

"No, I've missed a connection and am waiting at Horley for the next train to Gatwick."

"So, you are still coming? Any idea of what time you'll arrive?"

"Yes, I'm still coming and no, I'm sorry. I've got two more connections, Gatwick to Reading, then Reading to Oxford. I'll get there are soon as I can."

"Okay, we'll see you when you arrive. I'll let the principal know."

"Thank you. Goodbye."

The train for Gatwick arrived and again was quite full, so he stood in the aisle until he got there.

Trying to get off the train was a joke. There seemed to be hundreds of passengers trying to get on, while he and many fellow passengers were trying to get off.

"Excuse me," he said, trying to make his way through the crowd.

He finally made it to the escalator and as he made his way to the barrier found he had a queue of people in front of him. There was a problem with the automatic barriers, so they all had to wait to show the ticket man their tickets.

Could anything else go wrong? he asked himself, looking at his watch.

He finally made it and the ticket man said, "All done?" taking his ticket.

"No," said Sam, snatching back his ticket, "I'm going to Oxford."

"Down to platform five for the next train to Reading, then change there for Oxford."

"Thanks," Sam said, hurrying off. As he got down to the platform, he saw the nine twenty-seven pulling out. The next train to Reading would be at ten o'clock and didn't get into Reading until eleven nineteen.

Fine, he thought. *Oh well, hopefully there will be a train to Oxford when I arrive. I shouldn't be too late.*

With half an hour to waste, Sam desperately needed the loo, so went off in search of one. He had a problem with his prostrate and thought to himself how lucky he'd been that 'Arry had drunk his tea earlier; otherwise he'd never have made it 'til now. While he was there, he washed out his flask and cup thoroughly, then made his way to the nearest café to fill it up again. He then made his way back to platform five, found a seat, and sat down. He didn't have to wait long as it came in early and sat on the platform for ten minutes before it left. Sam got on and settled himself down in a one-seater to make sure he wouldn't have any unwanted company. The journey went without a hitch. Sam got out his flask, poured himself a cup of tea and settled down to read his favourite sports page on the back of his newspaper. It didn't seem long before he heard the announcement that the next stop would be Reading. He bundled everything up into his bag and got ready to get off. He then sought to find a guard on the platform to ask where the train to Oxford went from. That took some time, as there didn't seem to be many guards around. Eventually he found one, so made his way over there, which was a good five minutes' walk away, only to find he'd just missed one and the next one would be eleven forty-five and would get in at twelve ten. He sighed with relief and realised he'd have plenty of time to get to the interview. Thank God for Lucy! He went off to have a coffee in the station café. The smell of sizzling bacon tantalized his nostrils and made his salivary glands water, so he ordered himself a bacon butty. Thank goodness things were going his way at last. He studied the map Lucy had made for him and thought it shouldn't take over twenty minutes' walk to get to the college, so he'd get there on time. Twenty-five minutes later, he eventually found himself on the train to Oxford. Once there, he decided he had enough time to go to the toilet. Following the signs, he found a long queue of men and women waiting for the loo. If he hadn't been so desperate, he would have carried straight on to the college. Luckily, the queue started moving, when suddenly someone behind him stood on the back of his heel. He spun round in pain and pulled away to find that the heel of his shoe was hanging off. The lady behind couldn't apologize enough.

"I'm so sorry. I don't know what made me think you were going to move forward. Really, I'm very sorry," she cried out in great embarrassment.

27

Sam, being Sam, couldn't bear to see her so distressed, so tried to reassure her.

"It's alright, don't worry. It could have happened to anyone," he replied. Inside he was seething, but he couldn't do anything about it, so thought it was best to be gracious.

When he finally got into the loo, he had a good look at the heel. *It didn't look to safe,* he thought; *I must buy another pair for the interview.* As he went outside, he looked at the map and hoped he would pass a shoe shop on the way to the college. Having already phoned the college to say he would be late, he felt he had some time to spare.

He came out of the loo and the heel of his shoe made a slapping sound as he walked along. People looked at where the sound was coming from, and Sam felt very embarrassed. So, he went up to a man in the street and asked,

"Do you know where a shoe shop is?"

"Sorry mate, I'm just visiting."

He walked further and, as the flapping seemed to get louder, he stopped to have a look at it. As he bent over, he heard a voice say,

"Broken your shoe?"

"Yes. I'm going to an interview. I'm almost half an hour late and now my shoe's coming apart."

"If you go down there," he said, pointing, "it will take you to the centre of Oxford, you'll find something there."

"Thank you very much."

"No problem. Best of luck at the interview," he said, walking off in the opposite direction.

On the way, he saw a Chinese man having a cigarette outside his restaurant and asked him.

"Excuse me, I'm looking for a shoe shop. You wouldn't know where one was, would you?"

"Eh?"

"Shoe shop?" he repeated, pointing at his shoe.

The Chinese man called over a friend and spoke to him, pointing at Sam.

"Can I help you?"

"My shoe's broken; can you tell me the way to a shoe shop please?"

The man took him to the corner and said, "You walk here straight, okay?"

"Thank you," Sam said, and hurried off, panicking now about the time. Flap, flap, slap the heel sounded as he continued along. There was no sign of a shoe shop, so he asked another person.

"Excuse me, can you tell me where the nearest shoe shop is, please?"

The lady just shrugged her shoulders and turned away. *Obviously a foreigner that couldn't understand English.* He then spotted a town crier, but as he approached him, the whole of his sole came away from the shoe.

"Good afternoon, can I help you?" the town crier asked.

"Good afternoon. I need a shoe shop and directions to Jesus College, where I've got an interview."

"Go down Avenue 1, over there, and you'll find a shoe shop called *Clarks* they sell shoes."

"Thank you," said Sam, making his way over to the shoe shop. He went in and his hopes fell when he spotted the prices. Nothing was less than £75, he couldn't afford that.

Blast, he said, looking at his watch again, *this is ridiculous.* Just then, he spotted a cobbler. He rushed over and asked if he could stick his sole back on.

"I can stick it on for you, but it will mean you walking around for an hour with one shoe," he said.

"I haven't got an hour to spare. I'm going to an interview. In fact, I'm nearly an hour late," Sam explained in sheer panic. "All I need is a reasonable pair of shoes. I've got to get to this interview."

"You could try *Next,*" the cobbler suggested. "It's just around the corner," he said, pointing the way.

After thanking him, Sam rushed around the corner and, finding *Next,* went in and found some shoes at only £27.99. He knew Lucy would say he should only buy leather, but needs must. He heard a soft voice say,

"Can I help you?"

"Have you these in an eleven or twelve please," Sam said, handing him the shoes he'd found.

"I'll have a look for you," he replied, taking the shoe with him.

Five minutes passed before he came back. Sam was beyond worrying anymore.

"Sorry, I've been so long. I've found both the eleven and twelve," the sales assistant said, handing him over the shoes.

He tried the elevens on first, too tight, then the twelves.

"Great, they fit. I'll have them."

"If you'd like to come over to the till, please," the shop assistant led the way.

"Would you like the box?"

"No, a bag will be fine, thanks."

"Have a nice day," the assistant said, handing over the bag.

He paid the assistant and rushed off to change his shoes. Once outside the shop, he found a bin and placed the offending shoes, now inside the bag, into it. *This has got to be the worst day of my life,* he thought.

He turned the corner and nearly bumped into the town crier again.

"Look, I found some shoes," he said, "now can you tell me the way to Jesus College."

The crier turns to his friend and asks,

"Do you know the quickest way to Jesus College?"

"Yes, down Broad Street, then turn right into Turl Street," he replied.

At precisely one twenty-five, Sam walked into the college and up to reception.

"I'm Mr Walker. I've come for the interview as caretaker."

The receptionist looks down at the list and ticks him off.

"Ah, you made it then. Your interview was at twelve thirty. Where have your come from?"

"Eastbourne, East Sussex," Sam replied.

"That's a long way to come for an interview," she turned away, saying, "I'll be back in a minute."

She went off and then came back saying,

"I'm afraid you'll have a bit of a wait. He's just started interviewing another person and there's another three people for the job before you. Take a seat over there. Would you like a cup of coffee?"

Sam couldn't think of anything better and gratefully accepted her offer. As he sat there, he told the receptionist

31

about the day he'd had. She sympathised, and they ended up laughing.

"You are having a bad day, aren't you?" she pointed out.

Sam looked at the other guys waiting for the job and decided he was the oldest there.

"Hi, I'm Sam."

"Hi, I'm Jim. Sounds like you've had a bit of a day. Where have you come from?"

"Eastbourne in Sussex. Where do you come from?"

"I'm from Chester, born and bred there. Never left the place."

"Have you worked as a caretaker before?"

"Yes, but only for a year in a primary school. Couldn't stand it, right little blighters the kids were. The youngsters nowadays think they can do what they want and get away with it. I'm hoping that working with young intelligent adults will be a lot better. What about you?"

"Yes, I worked for six years at a primary school. Loved it, but had to go to Wales to look after my mum, who had dementia."

"Oh, sorry to hear that, mate. You married?"

"Yes, I've three children, all left home now. What about you?"

"The wife left me and took my two kids with her. I found out she had been having an affair with the teacher, a woman at that. That's why I'm looking for another job."

"That sounds awful. I'm sorry to hear it," said Sam.

"It's a bummer, but shit happens."

"I know, but I can't imagine what you must go through. Do you have access to the kids?"

"Yes, at the moment it's alright, but if I get this job, I'll only be able to see them on the odd weekends."

"How do you feel about that? How old are they?"

"Jill is seven and Tony is six."

"That's young. Won't you miss them?"

"Yes, I will, but I can't stay in a job with her having moved in with this teacher, who I'll see every day. It would kill me."

"No, I suppose you can't."

Just at that moment, the phone rang.

"James Henderson, they're ready for you now. Would you like to come this way, please?"

"Good luck, Jim," Sam said.

"Thanks mate, good luck to you too." Then he left.

The receptionist took him up the stairs and vanished around the corner.

Sam turned to the other two.

"Who's next then? "he asked.

"Me. I'm Tony," he said, putting out his hand.

"Hi, I'm Sam," he said, shaking his hand.

"I'm Fred," said the other guy.

"Where do you both come from?" he asked.

"I'm from Reading," said Fred.

"I'm from here, in Oxford," said Tony.

"Have either of you worked as a caretaker before?" Sam asked.

"I've worked in two nursing homes over the past ten years as a maintenance manager," Tony said.

"I've worked in Reading prison in the maintenance department for the past seven years," said Fred, "but they've just closed down the old place."

"That's interesting. My wife Lucy worked for a time in a young offenders' prison teaching English as a foreign language. Her Majesty's Prison Huntercombe in Henley on Thames. We lived in Pangbourne where I had started work as resident caretaker in a primary school in Pangbourne Primary."

"Really? That's interesting? How long was she there for?" asked Fred.

"Six years. She loved it. I thought she was mad at first and tried to point out all the dangers. She insisted there weren't any. We then moved to Pangbourne and after a year she left the prison and came to work as a teacher in the school I worked in."

"So, where did you live before Pangbourne?"

"We lived in Nettlebed. I worked as a self-employed painter, decorator and general maintenance for about seven years. It wasn't far for Lucy to get to Henley on Thames, but then I thought about a pension, so went for the job at the school."

"Blimey, you've done quite a few different jobs, haven't you?"

"Yes, I suppose so. Luckily, Lucy loves Oxford, her sister lives here and they're very close. They've missed each other since we moved to Eastbourne. She knows I don't like my present job in Eastbourne and saw this job advertised in the caretaker, so applied for it without telling me. I only heard about it on Wednesday."

"You're joking. What the hell did you say?"

"Well, I wasn't best pleased at first, especially as today is Friday the thirteenth. I can't stand doing anything on Friday the thirteenth. Everything is going to go wrong on that day. To be quite honest, it already has."

"Yeh, I overheard you telling the receptionist when you arrived. What an awful time you seem to have had. I certainly wouldn't have come for an interview if it was on Friday the 13th especially if I was as superstitious as you."

"To be quite honest, I wish I hadn't now," Sam admitted. "It's all been a waste of time so far and the interviews bound to go wrong too."

"Your luck's bound to change, mate," said Fred, trying to comfort him. "Surely, nothing else could go wrong."

"I must find a toilet," said Sam. "must have been all the coffee I drank today."

He asked the receptionist where it was and left to find it. On arrival, he opened the door to see two grown men snogging in the corner.

"Sorry," he said, going bright red, "just need to use the loo," and scuttled off into the nearest vacant compartment.

He felt mortified and sat for a while, hoping the men would leave before he came out. When he heard the door open, then close, he felt safe enough to wash his hands. The toilet was empty. He wondered to himself, *Were they masters or students? What had he come to?'*

As he arrived back, he saw Tony had gone. Just Fred and he left.

"How long do you think it takes for each interview?" he asked Fred.

"Between half an hour and an hour," he replied, "Why?"

"I thought we could have a bit of a walk to stretch our legs. What do you think?"

"Sounds good. Let's ask the receptionist first," said Fred, getting up.

"Great."

"Well, I wouldn't be too long," she said. "Don't go too far."

The two of them set off, glad to be out in the fresh air. They arranged the buildings around a vast square of grass. It was a lovely sunny day, and they walked around the circumference of the lawn. As they were on the home straight, Sam spotted the two men he'd seen in the toilet vanish into a nearby door. He told Fred what he'd seen, and both had a good laugh over it.

"I have a niece who's gay," said Sam. "Lovely girl. It's funny, but I don't look at her any differently than any other girl. I always thought I'd be homophobic, but I'm not. However, I find two men kissing strange. I still get embarrassed."

"Me too, but like you, I don't mind. Everyone to their own, I say."

As they arrived back, Sam spotted James coming from the area of the loo. He looked a bit dishevelled.

"Hey James, how did it go?" asked Sam, going after him.

James was now in tears. Fred excused himself, saying he was next in and had better go.

"What's wrong, James?" Sam persisted.

"They kept asking me questions about Julie, my wife. Was I homophobic? Would I find it difficult working alongside gay men and women? I said the issue was more that my wife had gone off with a woman. I did not know she was interested in women. It hurt a lot. Anyway, they said there were many gay people in Oxford, both students and tutors, and it sounded like I wouldn't be happy among them. It broke my heart. I've never thought of gay people in a bad way. In fact, I've never thought of them at all. Anyway, I ran out of the interview, so that's one less for anyone to worry about. I feel a right prat."

"James, look, I'm really sorry this has happened. You've had a rough deal. How about we keep in touch? Here's my number. I'll most likely be in the same boat the day I've had," said Sam, handing him a piece of paper he'd just written on.

"Cheers, mate, I really appreciate the time you've given me. Hope you get the job. I'd better get off. See you around."

Sam sat outside for a while thinking about what James had said and wishing he could have helped more.

As he went back in, Fred came out. He looked pleased with himself.

"Good interview?" asked Sam.

"Yeh, it went well, thanks."

"Good, I'm really pleased for you."

Just then the phone rang, the receptionist answered it, and after putting it down she said, "Sam Webber, it's time for your interview. Come this way." She took him up some wide wooden stairs. The whole place smelt of polish and looked like it had been there forever and a day. She stopped in front of a huge, panelled door and said with a smile, "Here we are, best of luck," then walked away.

Sam knocked at the door and heard a low voice saying, "Come in."

He entered a large room with enormous windows overlooking the gardens below. There was grand wood panelling on the walls, with several paintings of the college adorning them. A single man sat at a vast table and beckoned him to sit on the chair in front of them.

"Good afternoon, I'm Mr Clark," he said, standing up to shake Sam's hand.

"Good afternoon. I'd like to say how sorry I am for being so late. Unfortunately, I had a few problems on the way."

"Just a moment." Mr Clark left the room and called out something through to Sam. Sam, who hadn't worn his hearing aids, thought he wanted him to join him in the next room, so got up taking his bag and folder with him; as he reached the door, he heard him say, "Tea or coffee?"

"Oh sorry, coffee with two sugars, please." And scurried quickly back to his seat.

As Mr Clark brought in the drinks, the door opened, and another gentleman came over to Sam and shook his hand, saying, "I'm Mr. Bond, the director of accommodation. I hear you've had a few problems getting here today."

"Yes, it's been awful," Sam replied, and told them the story.

Everyone ended up laughing. Mr Bond looked at his watch and apologizing said he must go. He had an important phone call coming through.

"I'll leave you in Mr Clark's hands. Goodbye and good luck."

Mr Clark pulled out a folder and after rummaging through them, held up a paper in front of him, "I have a list of questions I ask all the applicants. First, what sort of experience do you bring to this job?"

"I worked as a residential caretaker in a primary school for eight years, so I have plenty of experience with minor electrics, plumbing, carpentry, gardening, decorating, ordering supplies, cleaning and security. I have also worked for the past two years as a maintenance manager in a nursing home."

"Good, that seems to cover a lot of the things we're looking for. Have you been on any recent awareness courses?"

"Yes, I've recently taken day courses at my present job in fire prevention, control of substances hazardous to health, safeguarding vulnerable adults, health and safety and infection control. I have all the certificates with me," he said, pulling them out of his folder.

Mr Clark took the certificates and looked through them.

"Good. Have you ever had to deal with a member of staff that puts you under pressure?"

"Yes, in the nursing home I work at. When doing, say, a painting job, this member of staff will always come to me and ask me to leave that job immediately to do something minor, like replacing a light bulb or change some curtains in the bedroom. I can't leave the job there and then, as it means tidying all my things away, because of health and safety. I have to explain again and again that I will do it when I have finished the job I'm doing before I go home."

"Alright. Do you prefer to work on your own or as part of a team?"

"I'm happy to do both. I have no preferences."

"Good. I'll give you a few minutes to tell me about yourself and why you want this job."

"Well, after working in a nursing home with people who have dementia and are dying for the past two years, I know now that I would prefer to work around young people again. I have a young outlook and get on well with youngsters. I have three children myself, ranging from twenty to twenty-seven who have all left home now. My wife has a sister who lives with her family in Oxford, so we know Oxford well, as we came to visit her frequently when we lived in Pangbourne."

At that moment, a wasp flew through the window and headed for Sam. After being stung badly by a swarm of bees once, he swiped the wasp as it came nearer. Unfortunately, as he swiped the wasp for the third time, he hit it straight into Mr

Clark's face, where it stung him on the side of his nose. Mr Clark got up howling and said, "Surely, you know to sit still when a wasp comes near you."

"I'm so sorry," Sam said, getting up. "It's just that I'm terrified of wasps. I got stung all over by a swarm of bees once. I'm really sorry, they panic me."

Mr Clark's nose was red and angry. The door opened and Mr Bond came in, looked at the red nose and said, "What's happened?"

Sam turned to look at him and said, "It's my fault. I swiped a wasp away from me and it's stung Mr Clark's nose. Really, I'm so sorry. I better go. Today's been one of those days and I won't waste another minute of your time. I'm really sorry for everything."

Sam left the room in a hurry. He was embarrassed and very red. As he turned left to get to the stairs, he bumped into a lady who lost her balance and fell over. He looked in total horror as a wig she must have had on was sitting to one side over her face. Mortified, he rushed over to help her up. As he bent over, he heard a loud rip. His trousers had split. He couldn't believe what was happening. *What next?* He thought.

"I'm so sorry, are you alright?" he asked, trying to put his back to the wall, to cover his favourite red Liverpool pants that must show through the split in his black trousers.

"No, I'm not you fool," she said, trying to straighten her wig. "Can't you look where you're going?"

"I'm really sorry," wishing for the millionth time that day that he'd never, ever come to Oxford for this blinking interview. "Can I get you a seat?"

"No, just leave me alone. I'll be alright with no help from you," she said, holding her head and hobbling away.

As he heard a noise, he looked around to see Mr Clark standing there, holding a handkerchief to his nose. Beside him stood a very concerned Mr Bond. They had looked on at the new situation in disgust and walked off in another direction.

"Well, I guess that means I don't get the job," Sam said to no one in particular.

He made his way down to reception and asked, "Have you got a safety pin? My trousers have split."

"It's certainly not your day, is it? Here are a couple of safety pins. Be careful that they don't open when you sit down on the way home. With your luck, I wouldn't bother to put them in."

"Thank you," Sam said.

He then left the building, clutching his bag to make his way home. With a very red face, he swore he'd never, ever, go back to Oxford. He hated the place and couldn't wait to get back to the peace and normality of his job in Eastbourne.

Once he got on the train and settled down, he delved into his pockets to find his phone. He had decided he would let Lucy know the outcome of his day. It wasn't where he normally put it, so he searched every pocket he had. Then he looked in his bag. It wasn't there either.

Flaming hell, where has that gone? he said out loud to himself. People in the carriage looked over at him. He felt himself go red once again.

"Sorry, I've lost my phone, and it's the last straw after a terrible day."

"Do you know your number, mate?" said a chap sitting opposite him. "I can ring it and see if it's somewhere you haven't looked."

"Thanks, it's 07563227566."

41

The guy rang it, but there wasn't a sound to be heard.

"Looks like you dropped it, mate."

"Yes, that's about right," said Sam.

"Would you like to use mine?"

"It's hopeless. I can't remember her mobile and we haven't got a home line," Sam tried to explain.

Friday the thirteenth was certainly an unlucky day for him. He got out his paper and read the sports page. A smile lit up his face. At least his favourite team were playing tonight, *Thank goodness for that,* he thought, feeling a little better. He got off at Reading and made his way over to the platform that left for Gatwick. He had about ten minutes before it left, so he went over to Smiths to get himself a cold drink, some chocolate, and a fishing magazine. Settling himself down, he got out his chocolate and magazine. *Heaven,* he thought. An hour later, he arrived at Gatwick, got off, and went in search of the next train to Eastbourne.

An announcement came over the Tannoy, telling the passengers that all trains were cancelled from Gatwick to Eastbourne. There was to be a bus service put on instead, due to disruptions on the tracks between Gatwick and Polegate. Would they please make their way to the entrance, where buses were waiting to take them on their onward journey? Once again, they said they were sorry for any inconvenience caused.

"Inconvenience?" he said, "I certainly feel inconvenienced."

Others around him agreed; but as they had no other choice, they made their way to the buses. Lots of people were phoning their loved ones to let them know why they were going to be late. He couldn't even do that. *Lucy would be worried sick,* he thought, *but what could he do?* What a day it had been. He decided there and then that in the future, when he felt sick of his job, he'd keep his mouth shut, and hopefully Lucy would never, ever, look for another job for him again. Eastbourne was a nice place, and they really weren't so bad at work. *I must look at the positives,* he thought to himself, *not the negatives.* That's what Lucy always told him. I'll never complain about my job again.